OCEANS AND SEAS OF THE WORL

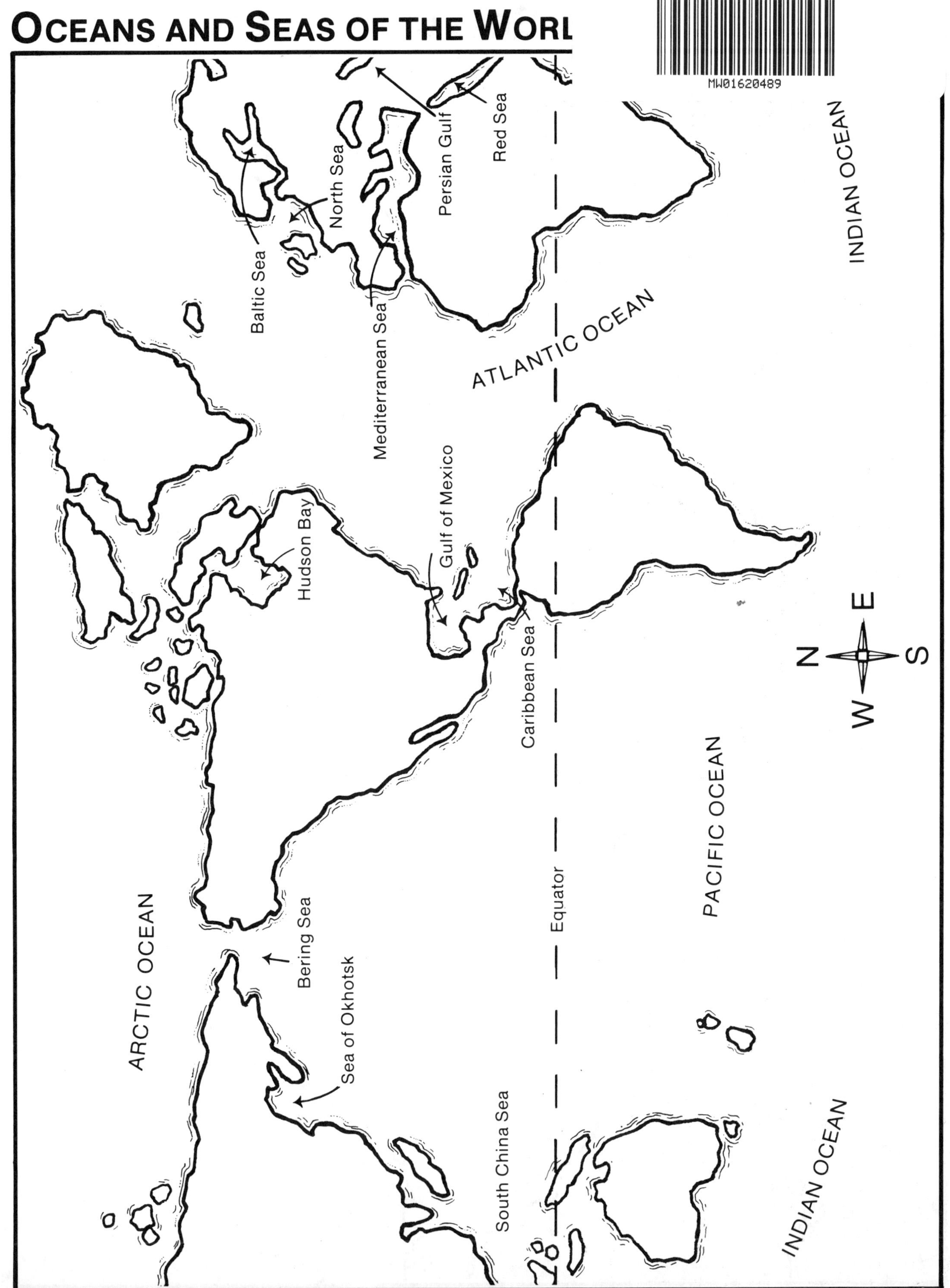

2 OCEANS AND SEAS OF THE WORLD

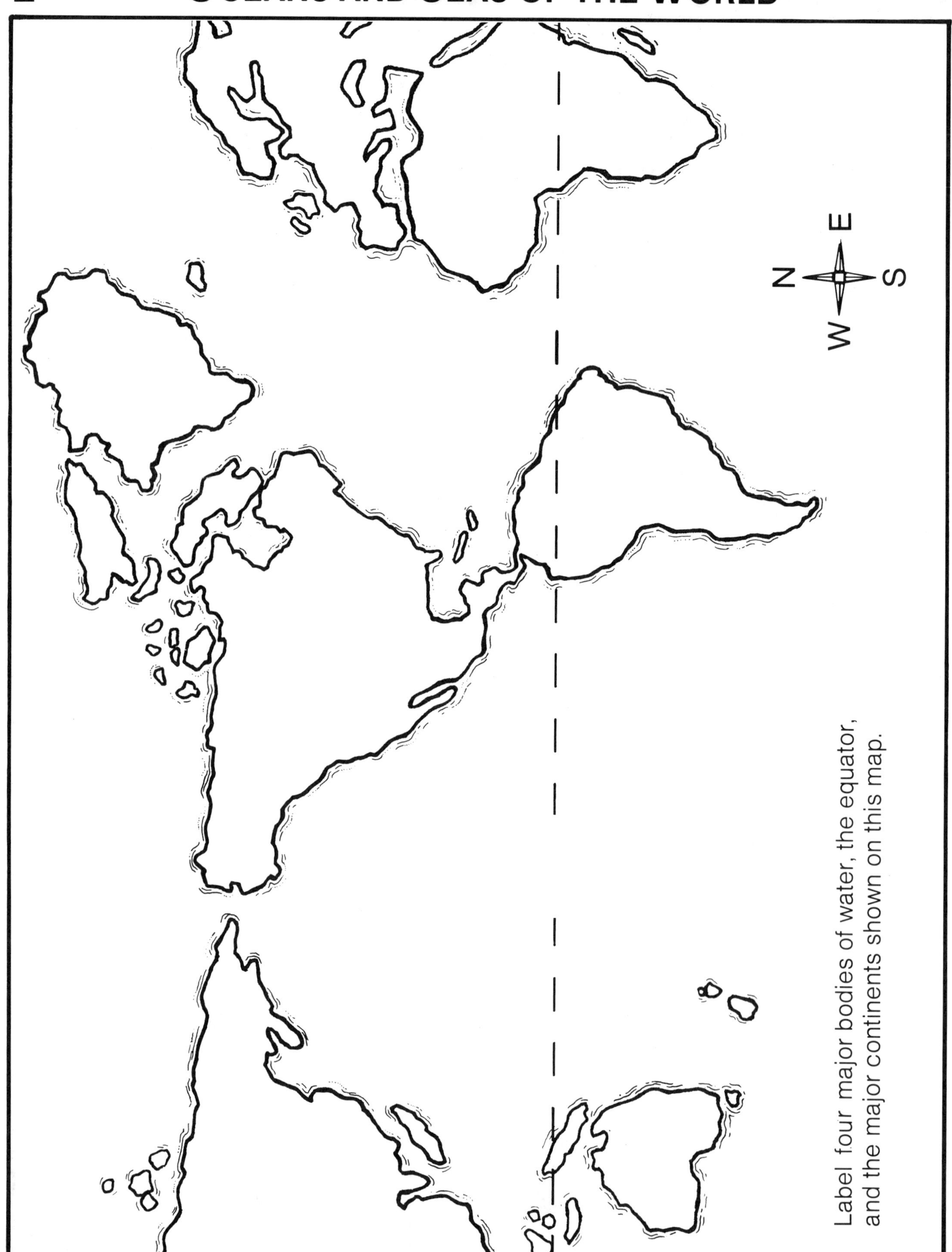

CHARACTERISTICS OF WATER:

THE EFFECT OF TEMPERATURE ON WATER 3

Water is one of the most remarkable substances in the universe. Try to discover some of the characteristics of water by completing the following activities.

A Fill a soft plastic container that has a tight-fitting lid (such as a margarine dish) completely to the top with water. Place the container inside a freezer until the water is frozen. Remove the container and observe its shape.

What happens to the size of water when it becomes solid? Does it expand (get larger), contract (get smaller), or stay the same? How do you know?

____

Try the above activity with a salt solution. Stir in as much salt as the water will dissolve. What happens? ______________________________

B Fill one pan with soil and another with water. Measure and record the temperature of the soil and water on the chart below. Heat each pan for several minutes. Measure and record the temperature after heating. Continue to heat each pan. Measure and record the temperature at intervals. Allow the materials to cool for five minutes and check temperatures. Measure again in another five minutes. What can you conclude about the temperature changes on land and water? ______________

____

	Beginning Temp.	Temperature After Heating ___ min.	Temperature After Heating ___ min.	Temperature After Cooling ___ min.	Temperature After Cooling ___ min.
SOIL					
WATER					

C Make a line graph of the results in **B**. Use one color for soil and a different color for water.

Beginning Temp.	After Heating ___ min.	After Heating ___ min.	After Cooling ___ min.	After Cooling ___ min.

Color Key
Soil ☐
Water ☐

CHARACTERISTICS OF WATER:

4 WATER AS A SOLVENT

D Water is a good solvent. It dissolves many materials. Most of the chemicals important to living things dissolve in water.

Compare the solvency of water with other substances. Measure equal amounts of water and several other liquids in glass or clear plastic containers. Stir equal amounts of salt in each. Start with small amounts of salt. Observe the rate that each dissolves. Some substances to use as solvents, in addition to water, might be alcohol, white vinegar, cooking oil.

Solvent	Dry Substance Added	Amount Added	Time Stirred	Description of Dissolving

Try the same experiment, but use different powders this time. Instead of salt, use powders such as corn starch, sugar, baking soda. Record your results.

____

Solvent	Dry Substance Added	Amount Added	Time Stirred	Description of Dissolving

BUOYANCY OF WATER

E Explore the buoyancy (boy-an-cy) of water (its ability to support objects). Carefully place an uncooked egg (still in its shell) in a dish of water. Be sure the water is

deep enough to cover the egg. Does the egg float or sink? ____________
Remove the egg and add salt to the water. Stir the solution and keep adding salt until the water seems saturated (It will not dissolve any more salt.). Place the same

egg in the salt water. Does the egg float or sink? ____________

CHARACTERISTICS OF WATER: EVAPORATION

F Place a large glass pan on top of a piece of black paper. Fill a small glass dish with salty water and place it in the pan. Place a larger glass bowl, upside down, over the dish of salt water so its rim rests inside the pan. Place ice cubes in a plastic bag and tie the bag shut. Put the bag of ice on top of the larger, inverted bowl. Put the experiment where the sun will shine directly on it.

The heat from the sun will be absorbed by the black paper and warm the water. The heated water will begin to evaporate (dry up) and rise and condense on the glass bowl. When enough water drops are formed on the bowl, they may run down the bowl into the pan. If not, run your finger across the inside of the bowl, collecting the moisture. Taste the water. Is this water salty? ________

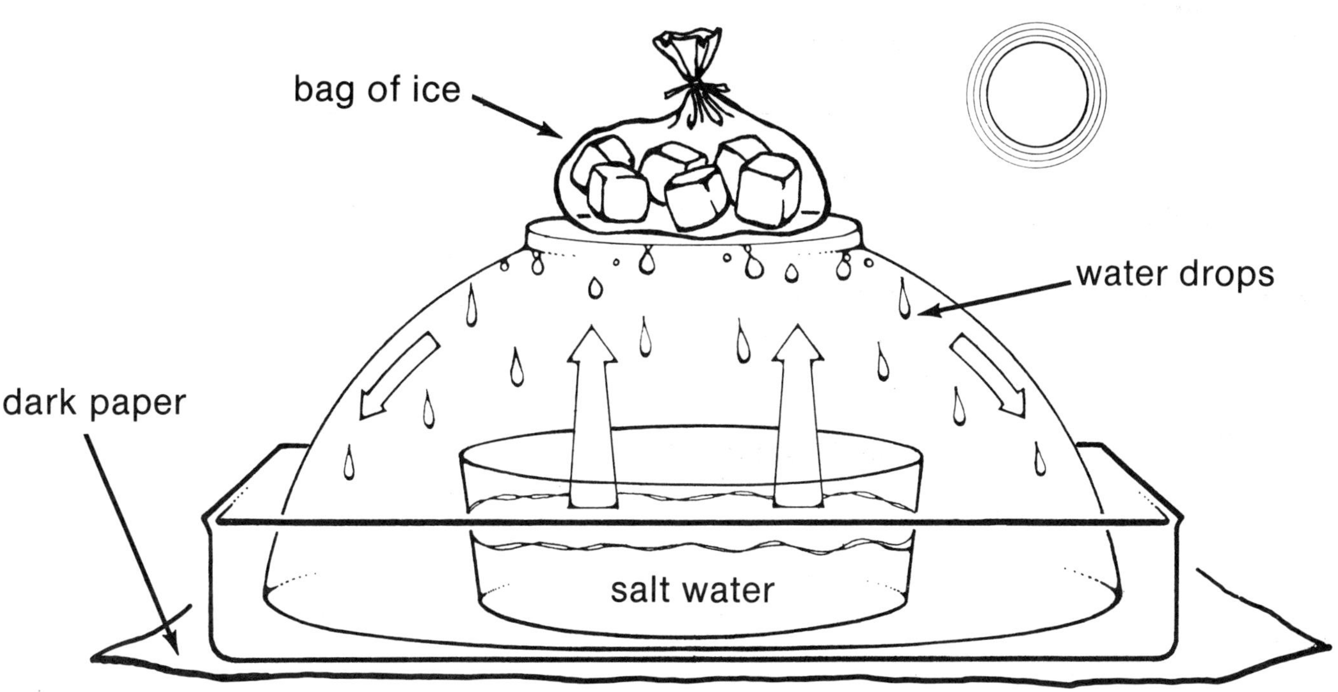

G Put five drops of salt water on a clean, flat piece of glass. Put five drops of plain water on another piece of glass or separate area of the same glass. Set the drops in the sun or under a light. Let the water evaporate (dry up).

What caused the water to evaporate? ________________________________

What happened to the salt when the water evaporated? ________________

How do you know? ____

Name some examples of evaporation that occur in your own life.

____

OBSERVING ICE

A

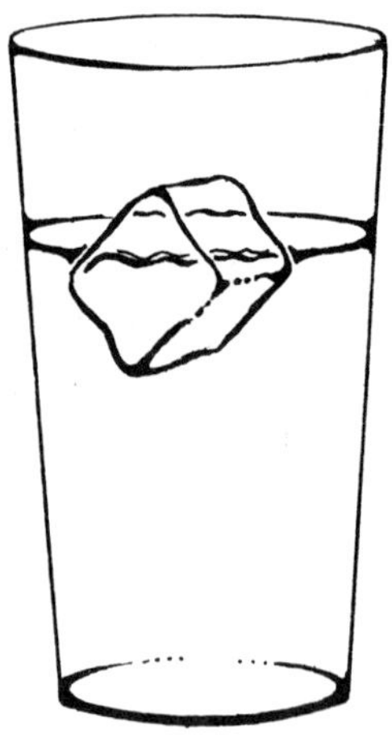

Observe an ice cube as it floats in a glass of water. How many different observations can you make? Write them below.

OBSERVATIONS

____

____

____

____

____

____

B Compare two ice cubes. Put one in a glass that is partially filled with a heavy salt solution. Put the other in a glass containing tap or distilled water. Use water that is the same temperature in both glasses. Put a thermometer in each glass. Add the ice cubes at the same time. Watch them and write your observations below. Keep track of the time it takes each cube to melt.

OBSERVATIONS

____

____

____

____

____

____

____

Which ice cube melted first? ______________________________

How long did it take to melt? ______________________________

How much longer did it take the second cube to melt? ______________________________

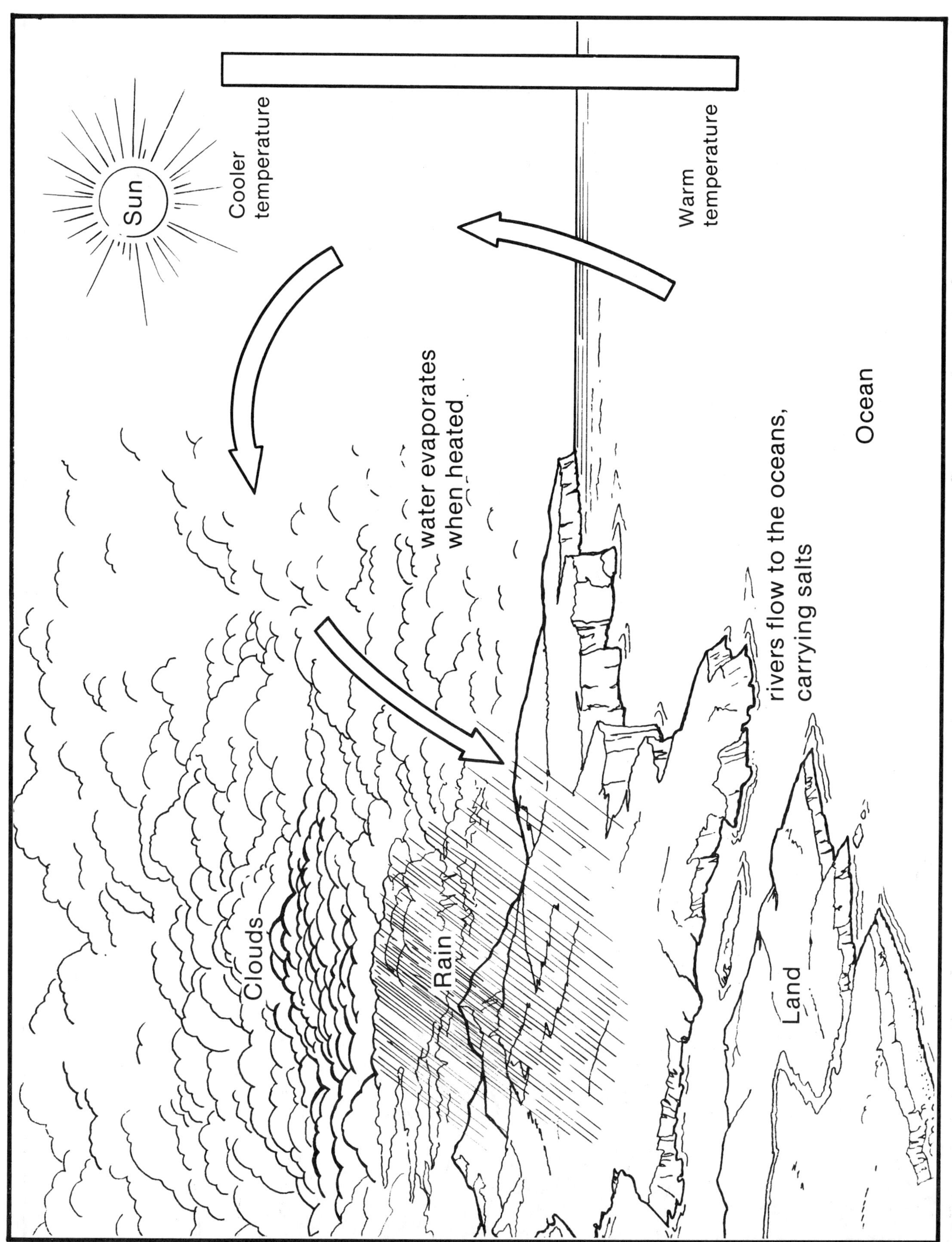

Sun
Cooler temperature
Warm temperature
water evaporates when heated
rivers flow to the oceans, carrying salts
Ocean
Clouds
Rain
Land

WATER CYCLE

Label the drawing of the water cycle. Use the
following words: clouds, cooler temperature, land,
ocean, rain, rivers flow to oceans, sun, warm
temperature, water evaporates when heated.

OCEAN FLOOR

Island
Island
Trench
Seamount
Guyot
Midocean Ridge
Rift Valley
Abyssal Plain
Canyon
Continental Slope
Continental Shelf
Continent
Estuary

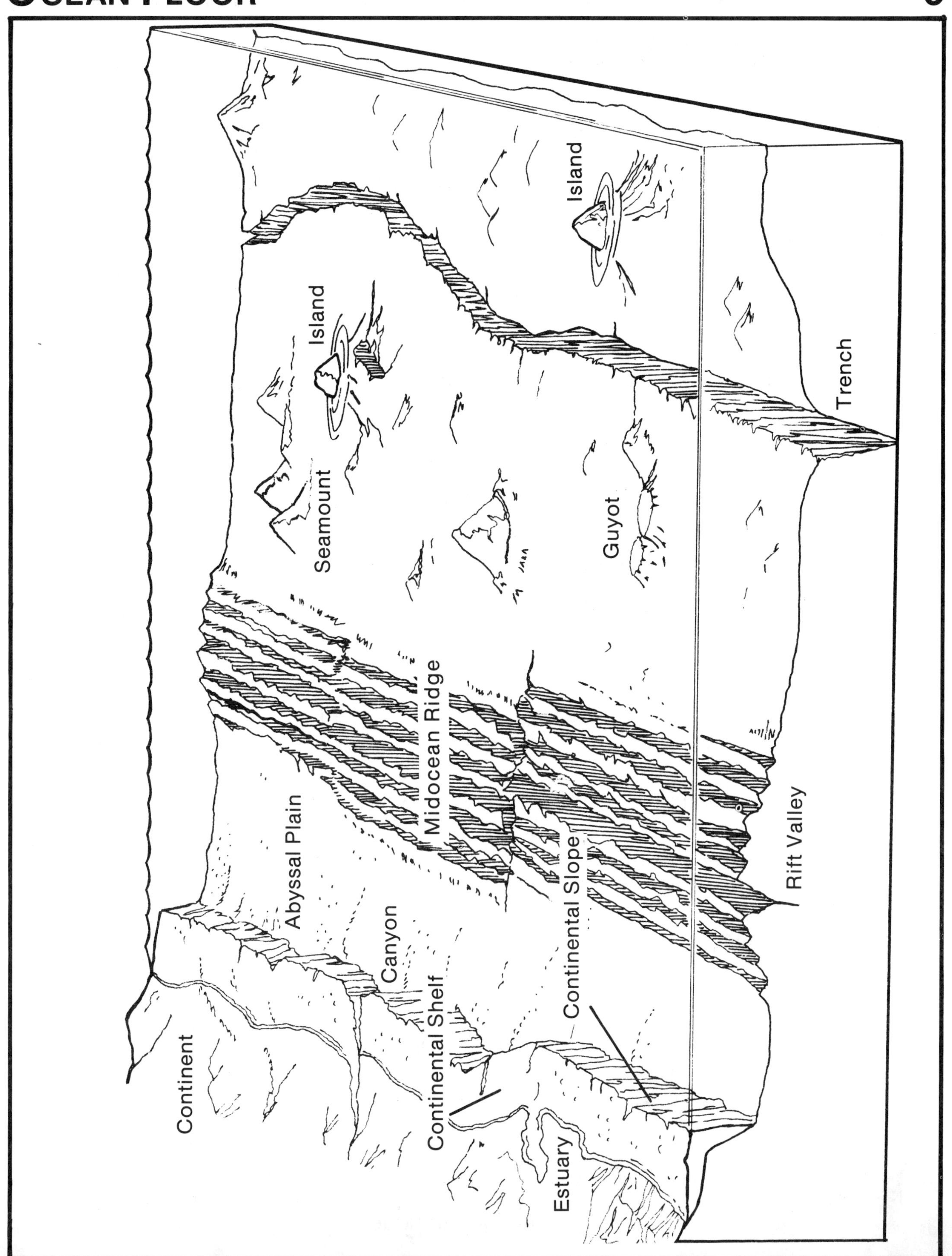

10 REVIEW: MAPPING OCEANS, CHARACTERISTICS OF WATER OCEAN FLOOR

1. Which changes temperature more rapidly, land or water? ______________________

2. Do objects float more easily in salt water or fresh water? ______________________

3. What happens to salt during evaporation? ______________________

____

4. Does evaporation occur when water is warmed or cooled? ______________________

5. When water becomes solid, what happens to its size? ______________________

6. What is a large, underwater mountain chain called? ______________________

7. Name four oceans of the world. ______________________

____

MATCHING: Match column B with column A. Write the correct letter on each line of column B.

	A	B
a.	continental shelf	___ water's ability to support objects
b.	continental slope	___ largest of earth's oceans
c.	seamount	___ flat region on ocean bottom
d.	trench	___ deepest part of the ocean
e.	abyssal plain	___ continuous circulation of earth's waters
f.	rift valley	___ water's ability to dissolve materials
g.	Pacific	___ steeply sloping underwater land
h.	water cycle	___ gently sloping underwater land
i.	solvency	___ underwater peak with round or irregular top
j.	buoyancy	___ large crack running down the middle of the midocean ridge

MAIN OCEAN CURRENTS

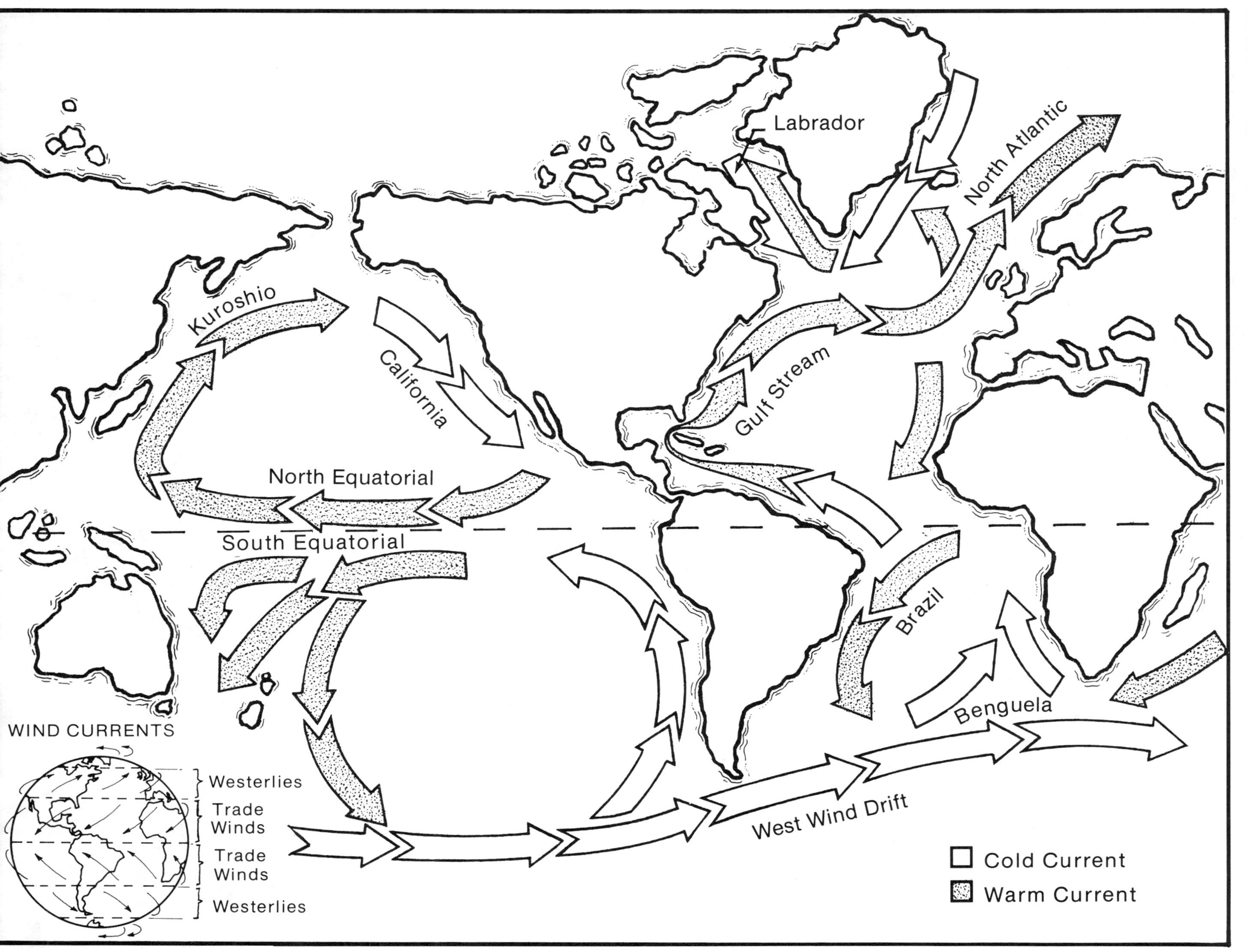

Main Ocean Currents

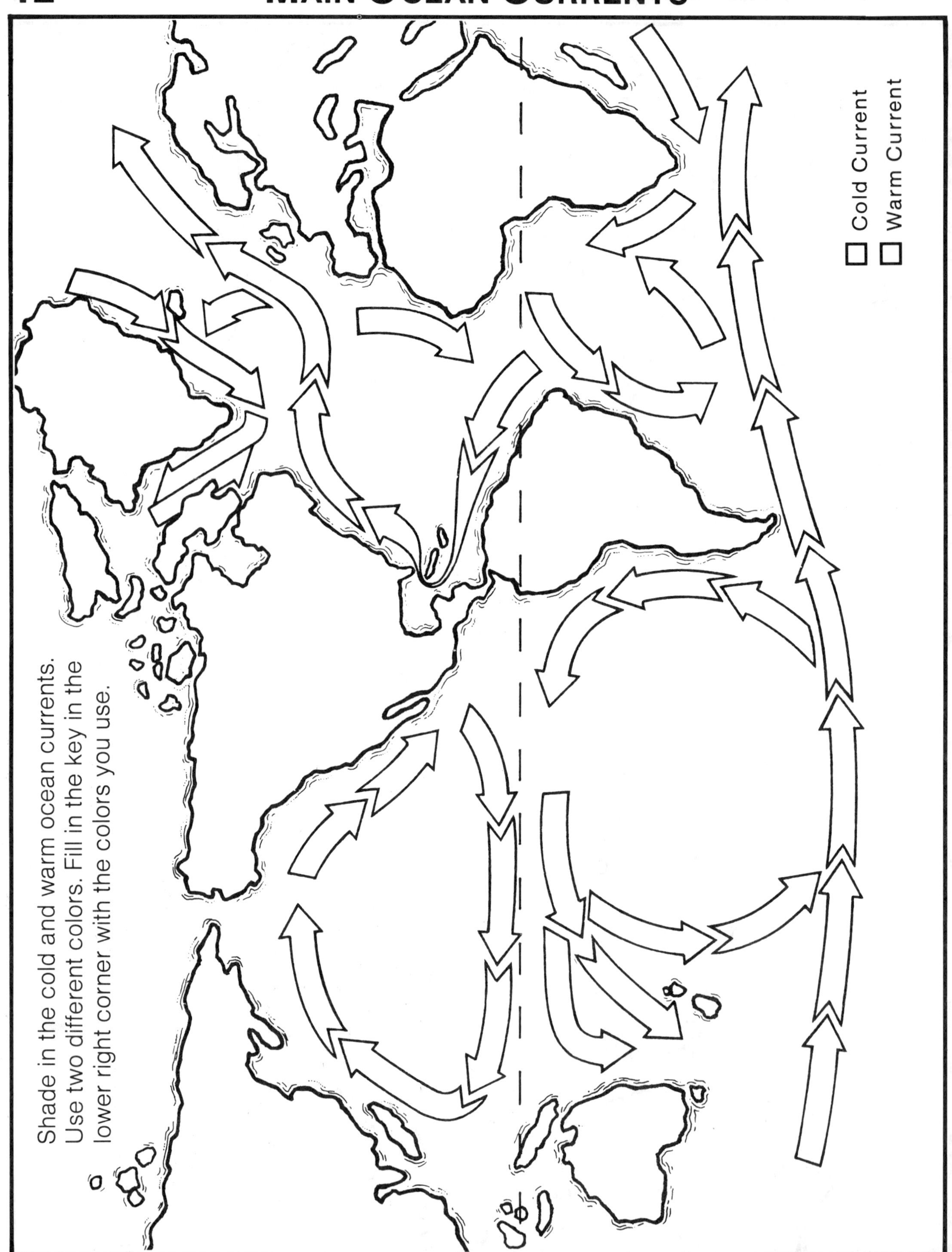

WATER CURRENTS

Use two glass jars that are identical, if possible. Their mouths should match each other exactly. Fill one jar with cold water and fill the other with hot, tap water. Color the hot water with food coloring and allow the color to spread evenly throughout the water.

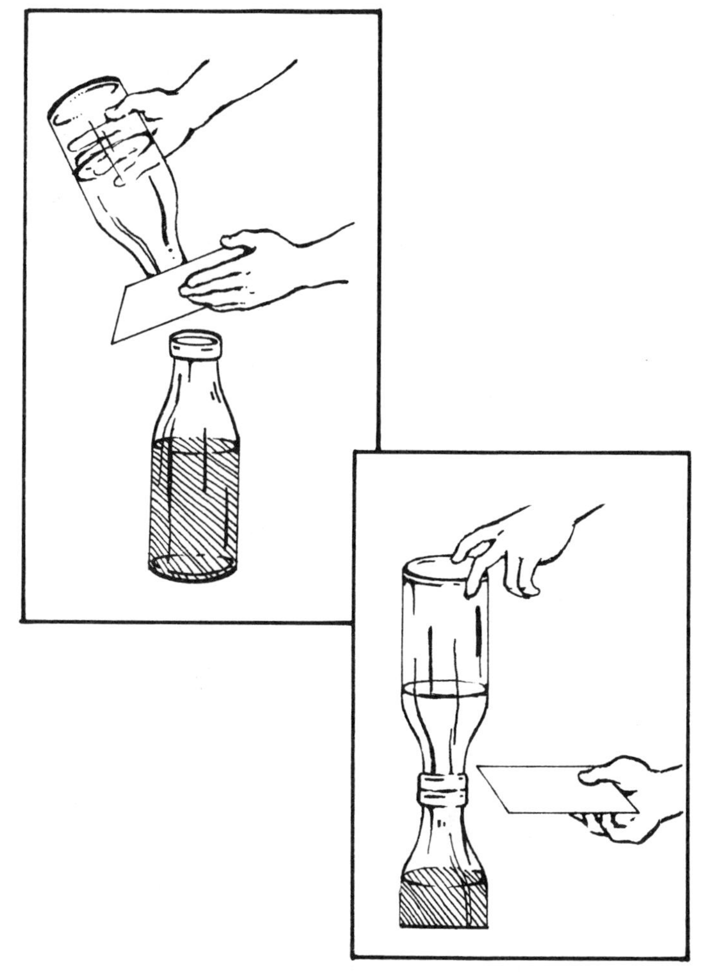

Then, using a thin piece of cardboard or stiff paper, cover the mouth of the jar containing cold water. Hold the cardboard tightly over the top of the jar. Carefully turn the jar upside down. Place it on top of the jar containing the colored hot water. Be sure that the mouths of the jars are directly over each other.

Slowly and carefully remove the cardboard. Ask a friend to help you. One person can hold both jars and the other can remove the cardboard.

What happens to the water? ____________

____

____

What does this say about water currents?

____

____

Reverse the experiment. Follow the same procedure described above, but this time, place the jar containing the colored hot water on top of the jar containing the cold water.

What happens to the water? ______________________________________

____

WAVES

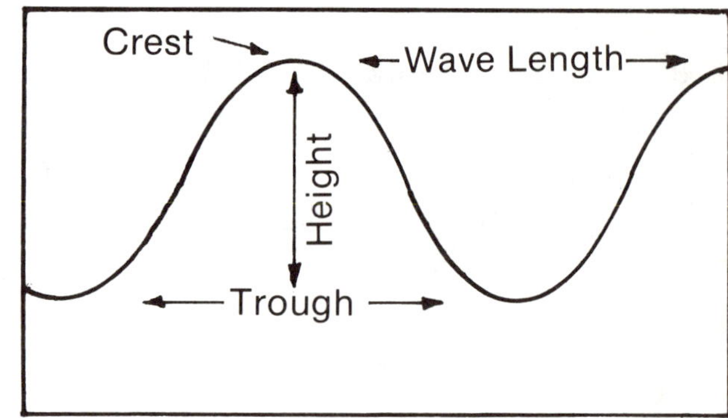

Waves are caused by winds, earthquakes, and the gravitational pull of the moon and sun. Most waves are produced as wind moves over the water, pushing against the surface. This causes part of the water to rise. The wind then pushes on the raised water and creates waves. Waves have two main parts: the crest and the trough.

When a wave gets close to land, its trough starts to drag on the bottom. This causes the trough to slow down while the crest still moves quickly. The crest gets higher and leans forward so far it eventually tumbles over. Then it is called a breaker.

On the diagram below, draw a wavy line where the water would be slowing down. Make an **X** where there is a breaker. Label a crest and a trough.

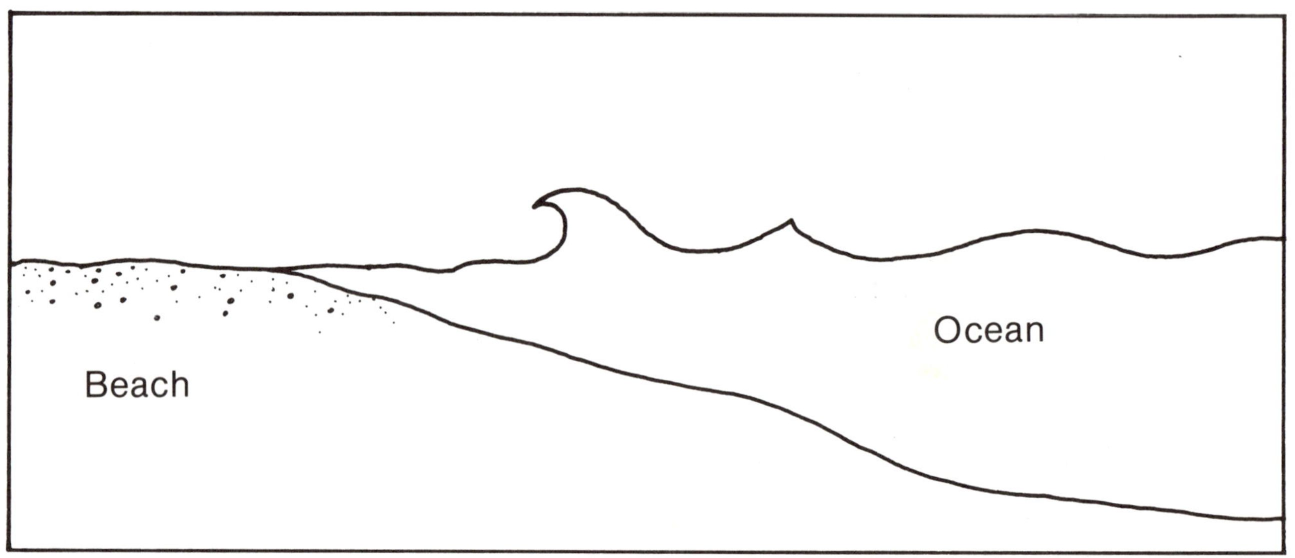

As the wave moves back into the ocean, it goes under the waves coming in and carries material from the shore. Waves also hit against cliffs of rock. They chip away and break up parts of the rock. In the drawing below, lightly color the area that has been removed from the cliff by the action of the waves. Color the area being built up by the deposit of this material.

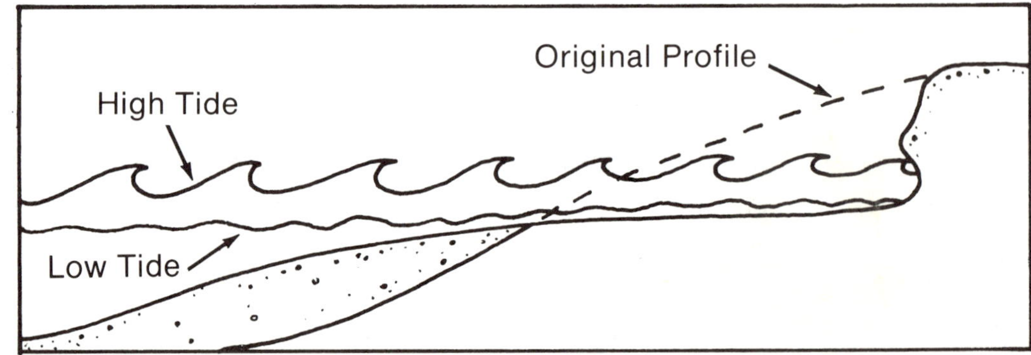

Find out about a special wave called a tsunami (tsŏŏ-nŏm-ē). Learn how surfers use the force of waves.

Pages 1—2 Ocean waters cover about 70% of Earth's surface. The oceans are really one continuous body of water. They are divided into four large areas. These divisions are not actual, but are names used to help people locate specific areas. In order of size, they are the Pacific, the Atlantic, the Indian and the Arctic. Sometimes the water around Antarctica is called the Antarctic Ocean. Each ocean contains smaller bodies of water closer to land called seas, bays or gulfs. The word sea is also used to refer to the ocean in general.

Seas may be classified into two divisions: enclosed seas and partly enclosed seas. Enclosed seas penetrate deeply into a continent and are connected with the open ocean by a narrow passage.

Partly enclosed seas are linked with the open ocean by broader entrances.

Pages 3—8 Water is one of the most remarkable substances in the universe. Many characteristics of water contribute to life. Water has one of the greatest transparencies to light; it has the greatest heat capacity of all liquids except ammonia. It conducts heat better than any other liquid and no other liquid has greater surface tension. It is the only substance occurring naturally as solid, liquid and gas on Earth's surface. Water is three times as abundant as all other substances combined. It dissolves more substances in greater quantities than any other common liquid.

Another property of water is its ability to support the organisms which live in it. This buoyancy allows huge animals, such as the whale, to survive. Their skeletons could not support their bodies on land. Most land plants and animals have strong supporting skeletons to hold them up.

Page 9 Some of Earth's greatest surface irregularities are beneath the sea. Just as continents have distinct features, so do the oceans.

In many places around the continents, the land gradually slopes under the water. This land is called the continental shelf. Continental shelves supply many resources. Great fisheries are there. Seaweeds are found, containing substances used in foods, drugs and commercial products. Oil and gas deposits are in many of these areas.

At varying depths, the gentle sloping of the continental shelves changes abruptly and becomes steep. Wherever this occurs, the increased steepness is called the continental slope.

Where the slopes end, the deep ocean floor, called the abyss, begins. Flat regions, called abyssal plains, may be found in all the oceans. Great mountains rise from the bottom of the ocean. Many are volcanoes. Some break the surface and form islands. A mountain chain, called the midocean ridge, runs through every major ocean. It is the longest mountain chain on earth. A large crack, a rift valley, runs down the middle of the ridge. The ocean contains a number of submerged isolated peaks, called seamounts, which have rounded or irregular tops. The deepest parts of the ocean are usually near the continents and are called trenches.

Much of the ocean floor is covered with sediment. Rivers carry sediments collected from the land and deposit them on the continental shelves. Some particles are carried farther from shore. Deep-sea deposits come from the continents and from the sea itself. Icebergs and wind may carry deposits out to the ocean, but most deep-sea sediments are made up of the hard parts of animals which die and settle to the bottom.

Interested students would benefit from further study of plate tectonics, including topics of continental drift, sea floor spreading, earthquakes and volcanoes.

Pages 11—13 Water moves about in the ocean in streams called currents. The spinning of Earth causes the air around it to move, creating wind. The wind moves over the ocean surface and pushes against the ocean water in large circles. These circular currents move clockwise in the Northern Hemisphere and counter-clockwise in the Southern Hemisphere.

At the Equator, the ocean water is warmer than it is at the poles. Since cold water is heavier, the colder water of the polar regions moves to the ocean bottom. It slowly moves toward the Equator as the warmer water moves to replace the sinking cold water. The movement of cold and warm water in this way causes currents which circle the globe.

Page 14 In an ocean wave, water moves up and down. There is no forward motion of water as the wave moves. It is similar to the motion made by a rope tied to a tree. If you shake the loose end of the rope, it will go up and down, but the rope itself will not move forward.

Tsunamis are seismic waves because they originate with some sudden rapid movement of the Earth's crust, such as an earthquake or an underwater landslide. They are very long waves that travel at great speed. As the waves approach shore, however, they slow down and the water piles up. The waves may form a wall of water as tall as a building.

Pages 15—18 The waters of the ocean sometimes come high up on the shore. At other times, the ocean is much farther out on the beach. These forward and backward motions of the ocean occur daily and are called high tides and low tides. To understand these tidal patterns, students need to know about the movements of the Earth, sun and moon and the unseen force called gravity. Gravity holds the Earth, sun and moon in their places. It also holds everything, including ocean waters, down to earth. The sun and moon both pull Earth toward them by their gravitational force. This pull of gravity is an important part of producing the tides.

Although the moon is not as large as the sun or Earth, its gravitational force is felt strongly on Earth because it is more than 200 times closer to Earth than the sun. The moon pulls hardest on the part of Earth nearest it. The pull lifts the water and causes it to bulge out toward the moon. This is called a tidal bulge. Where the bulge is greatest is high tide. As the moon circles Earth, it pulls the water in different parts of Earth into high tides. As the moon pulls with its gravitational force, there is an equal force called centrifugal force acting in an opposite direction to fling Earth away. Water bulges on the side facing the moon, and another bulge of the same size appears on the opposite side.

When the sun and moon are pulling on Earth at right angles, neap tides are produced. In neap tides, the range between the high and low tides is not very great. When the sun and moon are in line with Earth, spring tides, tides of higher than average range, occur. Spring tides and neap tides develop twice each month throughout the year.

Pages 20—24 Life in the oceans is characterized by great diversity. There are over 20,000 kinds of fishes alone. Both plants and animals can be found in abundance. Plants live wherever there is sunlight, usually near the surface. They do not live in deep, dark waters. Animals, however, exist everywhere — from the surface to the deepest parts. These animals range in size from the largest animal known (the blue whale) to microscopic one-celled plankton, on which almost all living things in the ocean depend.

The illustrations on pages 20 and 22 can help students become familiar with a few of the well-known representatives of the many plant and animal groups that live in the ocean. Encourage students to research the characteristics of those pictured. Which animals feed on others? Classify the animals into two main groups: vertebrates (having a backbone or spine made of cartilage, spinal cord and brain) and invertebrates (without a backbone). Research the process known as bioluminescence. Which animals pictured have bioluminescence? The study of ocean life is an excellent way for students to develop research and reporting skills. Sea life study can lend itself to many related art and creative writing activities.

Pages 25—27 Information about the ocean is gathered by many methods. Among these is the echo sounder which, when on a ship, sends out sounds which travel through the water until they hit the ocean bottom. Then the sounds bounce back to the ship. The time it takes for the sound waves to hit the bottom and return is measured. Oceanographers can figure out how far the sound traveled. Then they know how far down it is to the bottom.

One way of finding out about the composition of the ocean floor involves knowledge of refraction (light bending as it passes from one substance to another). Sound waves are bent in much the same way. A charge of explosives is set off. Since shock waves move through different materials at different rates, the structure of the ocean floor can be determined by comparing known speeds with those recorded by the investigators.

To find out about sediments on the ocean bottom, a long hollow tube, called a corer, is lowered and drilled into the sediments. The hollow part of the tube fills with sediment, is brought back to the surface, opened and studied.

Scientists have many specialized tools to help them collect data and study various aspects of the ocean. Oceanographers call upon knowledge from numerous sciences including geology, chemistry, physics and biology.

Men have been diving and exploring underwater for many years. Two major problems with such endeavors have been to provide an air supply and to withstand the pressures of the deep. Equipment that is available today has overcome these obstacles to varying degrees.

The aqualung, invented in 1943, is an air tank worn on the diver's back with a hose connecting the tank to the diver's mouth.

Deep-diving submersible vehicles have made almost every part of the ocean accessible to observation. The Trieste, operated by the US Navy for research, is a bathyscaph that set the world record for manned deep-sea dives when, in 1960, it carried two men to a depth of about 7 miles beneath the surface of the Pacific Ocean.

Most submersible vehicles are manned submarines capable of vertical and horizontal movement by self-contained power. They may have observation windows, externally mounted mechanical arms, and various attachments for collecting specimens.

This topic can be rather technical, but is well worth spending the time on additional investigation by students who might be interested.

ANSWERS

Page 2
Atlantic, Pacific, Indian, and Arctic Oceans
Asia, Australia, North and South America, Europe and Africa

Page 3
Water expands when it freezes. The container should bulge slightly when the water is frozen.

The salt water may not freeze solid.

The soil (land) will change temperature faster than water.

Page 4
The uncooked egg will sink at first. As salt is added, the egg will begin to float.

Page 5
The water will not taste salty. Salt is left behind during evaporation.

Heat from the light or sun caused evaporation. The salt was left behind. This may be evident by residue seen on the glass and by tasting.

Students can moisten a finger, run it over a place where there was a water drop, then taste their finger. The places where salt water was dropped will taste salty.

Page 6
Some observations might include ice floats, more of the ice is below the water, bubbles move up from the bottom, ice melts unevenly and ice

is clear around the edges and frosty in the middle.

Observations of salt and fresh water might include the fact that the temperature goes down farther in fresh water, the cube rises higher in salt water, and the temperature goes down quickly at first, then stops.

Page 10

land salt water It is left behind.
when water is warmed
It expands.
midocean ridge
Pacific, Atlantic, Indian and Arctic Oceans

J	I
G	B
E	A
D	C
H	F

Page 13

The cold water will sink to the bottom jar. The colored water will then be distributed throughout both jars.

It duplicates the movement of water causing currents that circle the globe.

When hot water is placed on top of cold water, the two bottles will retain their original color. The waters won't mix.

Page 14

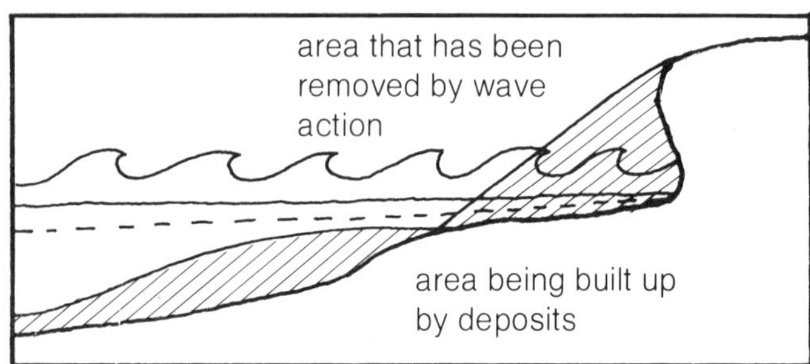

Page 15

365¼ days	1 year
24 hours	day

Page 16

365¼ days
29½ days
rotation of Earth on its axis
92,760,000 miles

revolves	sun
rotates	axis
revolves	

Page 18

A. spring — The sun and moon are in line with Earth.
B. neap — Sun and moon are pulling on Earth at right angles.

Page 19

cold water
The trough slows down while the crest moves quickly and tumbles over.

wind, earthquakes, gravitational pull of moon and sun

daily forward and backward motion of the ocean
gravitational pull of the sun and moon
Northern
23½°
the lifting of water caused by the gravitational pull of the moon
crest and trough

revolution	Humboldt
rotation	currents
29½ days	Westerlies
spring tide	crest
Gulf Stream	gravitational pull

Page 24

plankton-S	barnacles-S	lobster-S
snails-S	starfish-S	seaweed-S
jellyfish-S	shark-D	
tuna-D	squid-D	

Page 27

Self-Contained Underwater Breathing Apparatus
inability to breathe and to withstand the pressures of deep water

Rubber suits and flippers aid divers in underwater movement.

Page 28

bathyscaph
release of ballast
Water is allowed to enter certain compartments in the float.
7 miles
the float

F	F
F	T
F	T
T	F
F	T

Movements of Earth

Demonstrate these movements. You will need three people, a small lamp with shade removed, a globe, and a small ball.

Clear an area of the room large enough to move around (9′ x 6′). Place a piece of tape on the globe near where you live. Plug in light. Have one person hold it and another person hold the globe. Darken the room a bit.

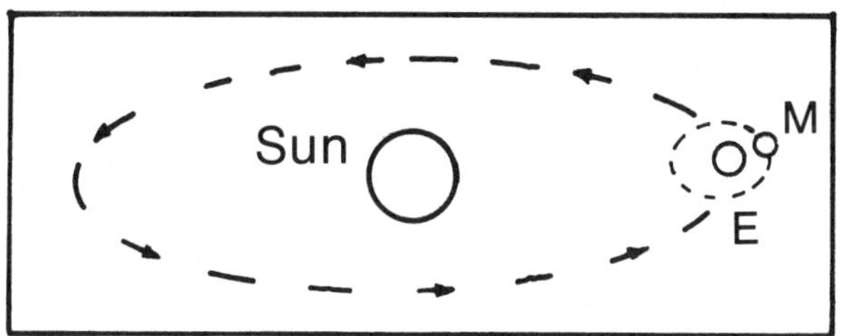

Movement of Earth and moon

A Show Earth's movement around the sun by walking the globe around the light. Try to keep the globe slightly tilted on its North-South axis. It takes Earth approximately one year (365¼ days) to make one trip (revolution).

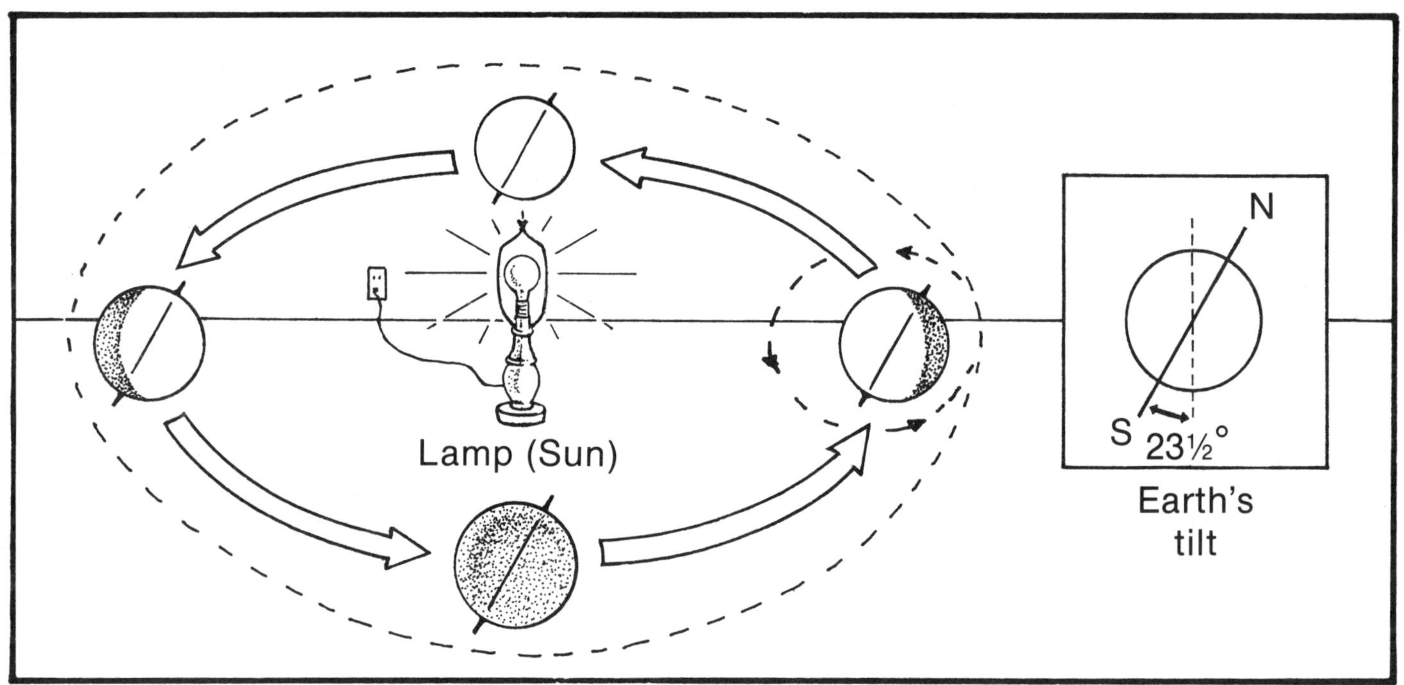

The dotted line that represents Earth traveling, in orbit, around the sun takes

__________ days. In terms of our calendar, that represents ___ year(s).

B Now, add the second motion that Earth makes. Spin (rotate) the globe on its axis from West to East. It takes approximately 24 hours for one complete turn. Walk around the light (sun) again, this time rotating the globe as you go.

The dotted line that represents the West-to-East rotation of the globe on its axis

takes _____ hours. In terms of telling time, that represents ___ day(s).

MOVEMENTS OF EARTH continued

C While Earth is rotating and making an orbit around the sun, the moon is orbiting around Earth once each month (about every 29½ days). Have the person holding the small ball (moon) join the Earth's trip around the sun. The moon will move faster around the Earth than the Earth moves around the sun. Try to keep distances in mind, although you need not try to represent them. The sun is 93,000,000 miles from Earth. The moon is a little under 240,000 miles away.

D Repeat these "trips" several times, carefully observing where the light falls on the globe and the relative movements of these three objects. In addition to the movements represented so far, the Earth, sun, and moon are all traveling together through space. It may be a little complicated to actually add this to the demonstration, but at least be aware that it happens.

1. How long does it take Earth to make one revolution around the sun?

   ____

2. The moon rotates around Earth every __________________ .

3. Which movement of Earth gives night and day? ____________________________

   ____

4. Approximately how much farther from Earth is the sun than the moon?

   ____

5. The Earth __________ around the __________ .

6. The Earth __________ on its __________ .

7. The moon ________________ around Earth.

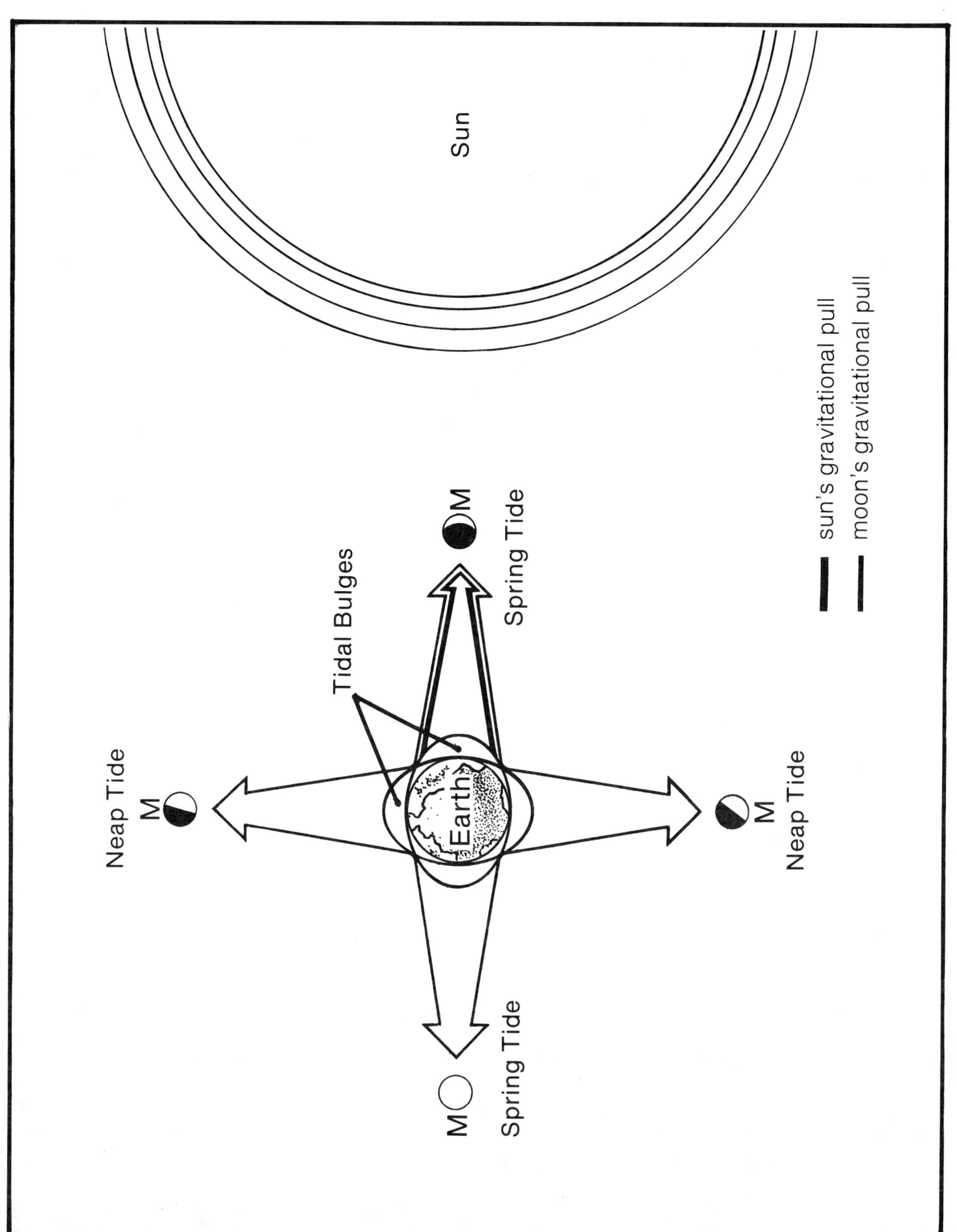

Sun
sun's gravitational pull
moon's gravitational pull
M
Spring Tide
Tidal Bulges
Neap Tide
M
Earth
M
Neap Tide
Spring Tide
M

UNDERSTANDING TIDES

Form a ball out of cotton. Place a rubber band around the ball just tight enough to fit, but not so tight that it destroys the round shape of the ball. On opposite sides of the ball, pull the rubber band and a little of the cotton between the thumb and index finger of each hand. Look at the resulting shape of the ball. This is somewhat like the pull of moon's gravity on Earth.

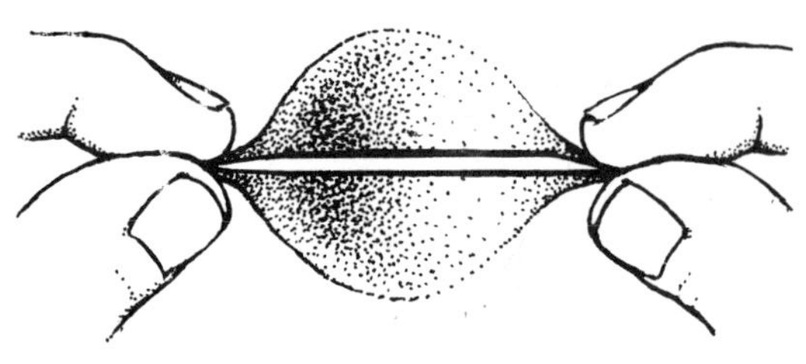

When the sun and moon are pulling on the Earth at right angles, neap tides are produced. When the sun and moon are in line with Earth, spring tides occur. Study the diagram. Complete exercises A, B, and C.

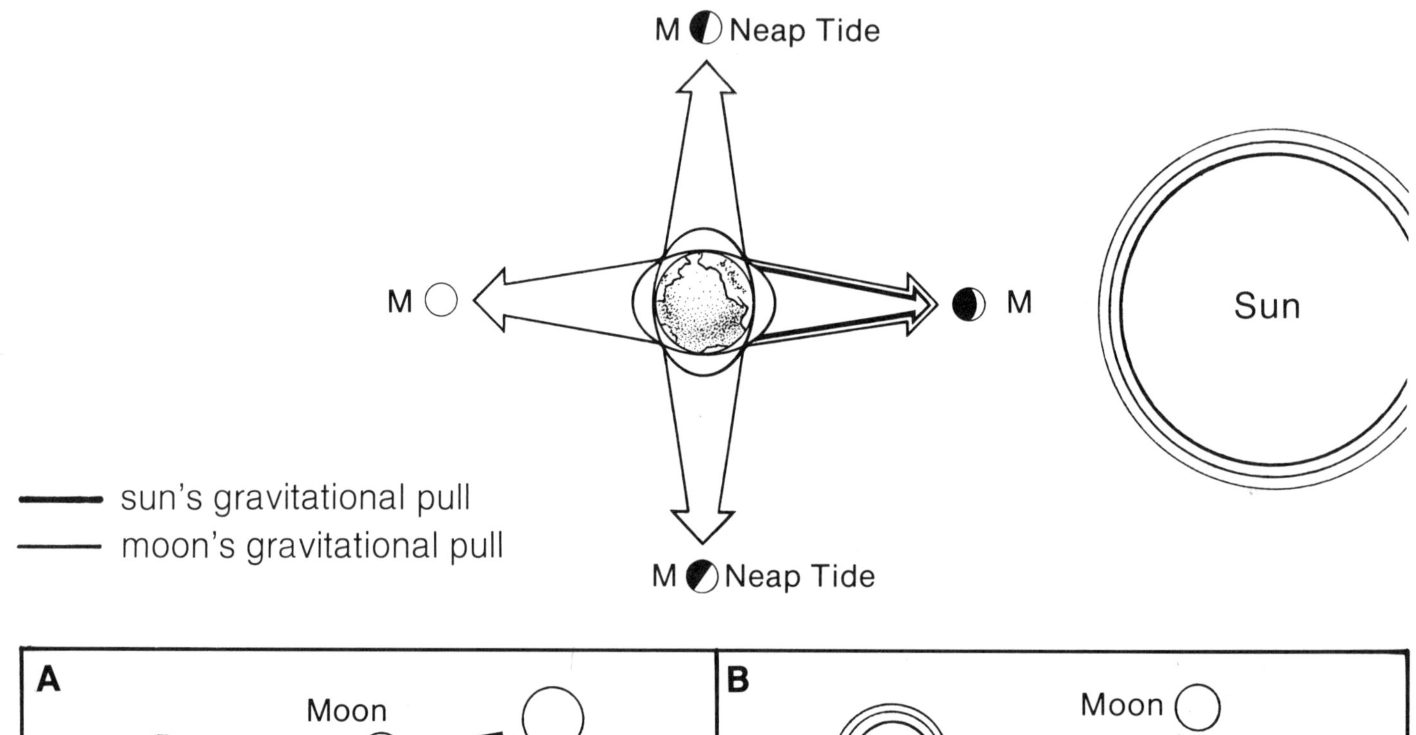

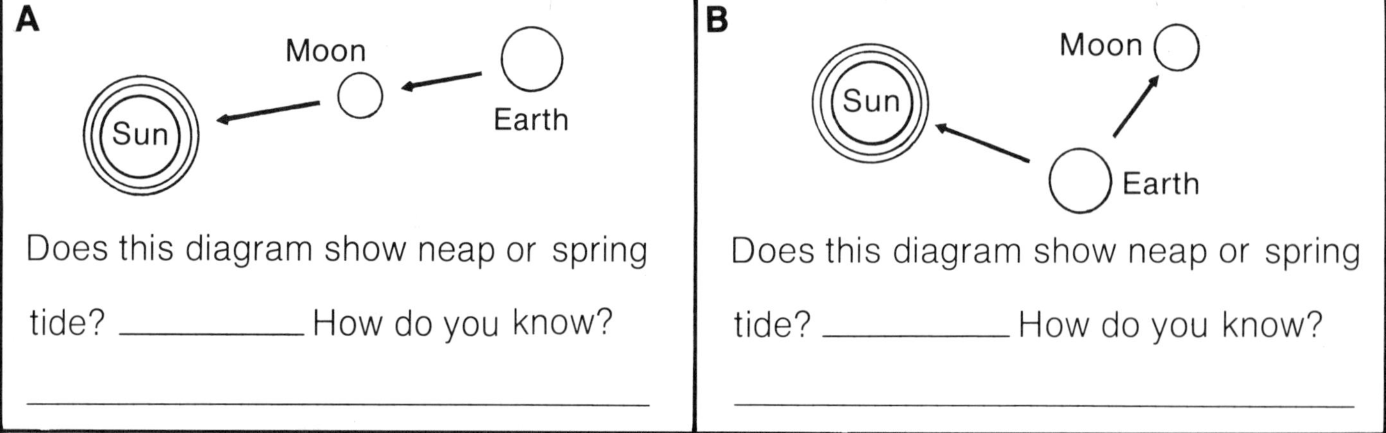

A Does this diagram show neap or spring tide? __________ How do you know?

____

B Does this diagram show neap or spring tide? __________ How do you know?

____

C Label the tidal bulges on the illustration.

REVIEW: WAVES, CURRENTS, TIDES

1. Which is heavier, cold water or hot water? ____________
2. What causes a wave to break? ____________
____
3. What produces waves? ____________
____
4. What is a tide? ____________
____
5. What causes tides? ____________
6. In which hemisphere do currents flow clockwise, Northern or Southern? ____________
7. How much does Earth tilt on its axis? ____________
8. What is a tidal bulge? ____________
____
9. Name two parts of a wave. ____________

MULTIPLE CHOICE: Choose the correct answer and underline it.

1. Earth's travel around the sun is called ________.
   rotation — revolution — gravitation
2. The spinning of Earth on its axis is called ________.
   rotation — orbiting — revolution
3. The moon travels around Earth once every ________.
   year — two weeks — 29½ days
4. When Earth, moon, and sun are in line with one another, a ________ occurs.
   neap tide — spring tide — current
5. A current that flows past the eastern coast of the United States is the ________.
   Gulf Stream — North Atlantic — West Wind Drift
6. A cold current that moves along the western coast of South America is the ________.
   Brazil — West Wind Drift — Humboldt
7. Temperature differences of the water in the ocean cause ________.
   currents — winds — waves
8. Winds that blow over most of the United States are called ________.
   Easterlies — Westerlies — Trade Winds
9. The highest part of a wave is its ________.
   bulge — trough — crest
10. Tides are produced primarily by ________.
   currents — salinity — gravitational pull

20 LIFE IN THE OCEAN—SHALLOW WATER

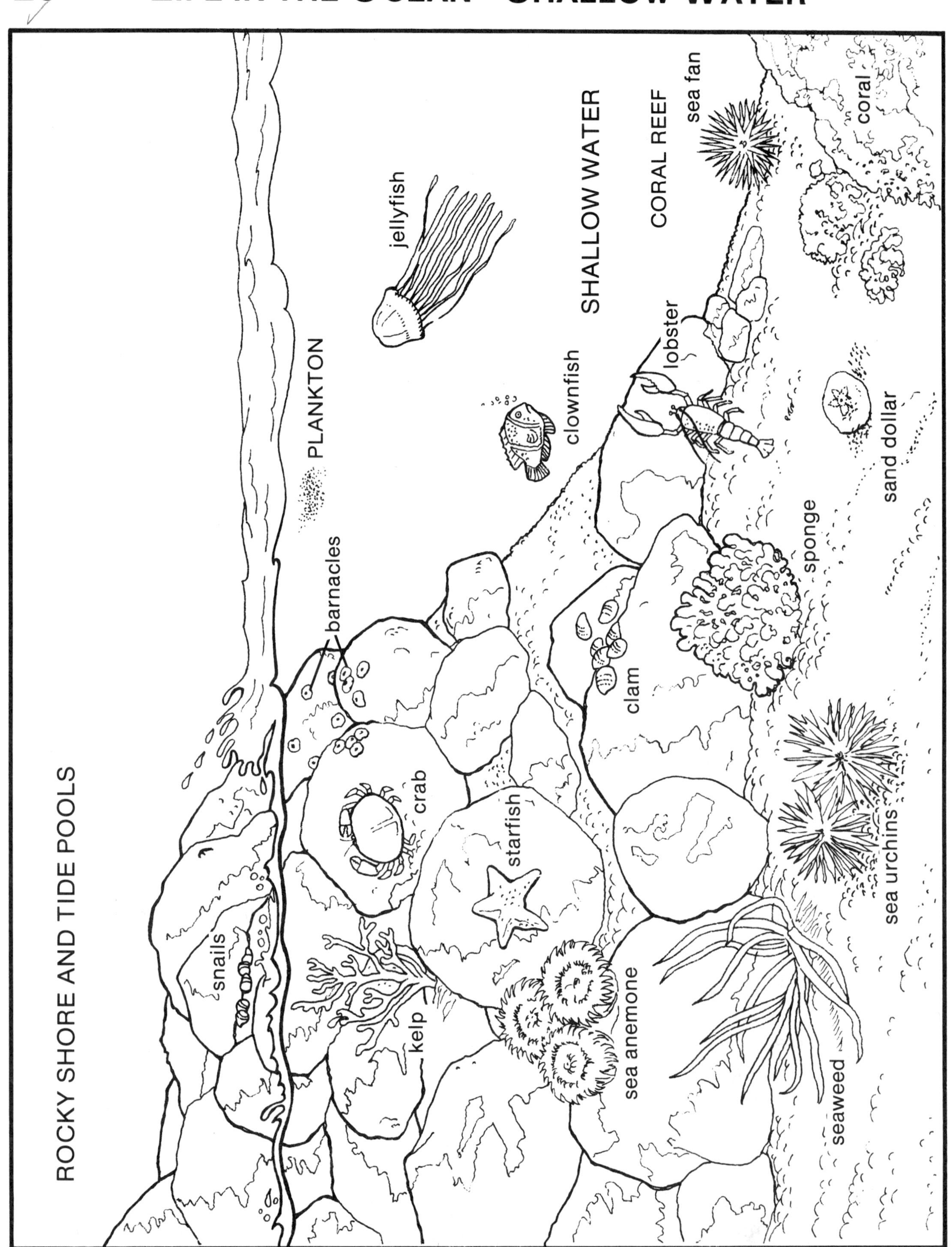

LIFE IN THE OCEAN—SHALLOW WATER

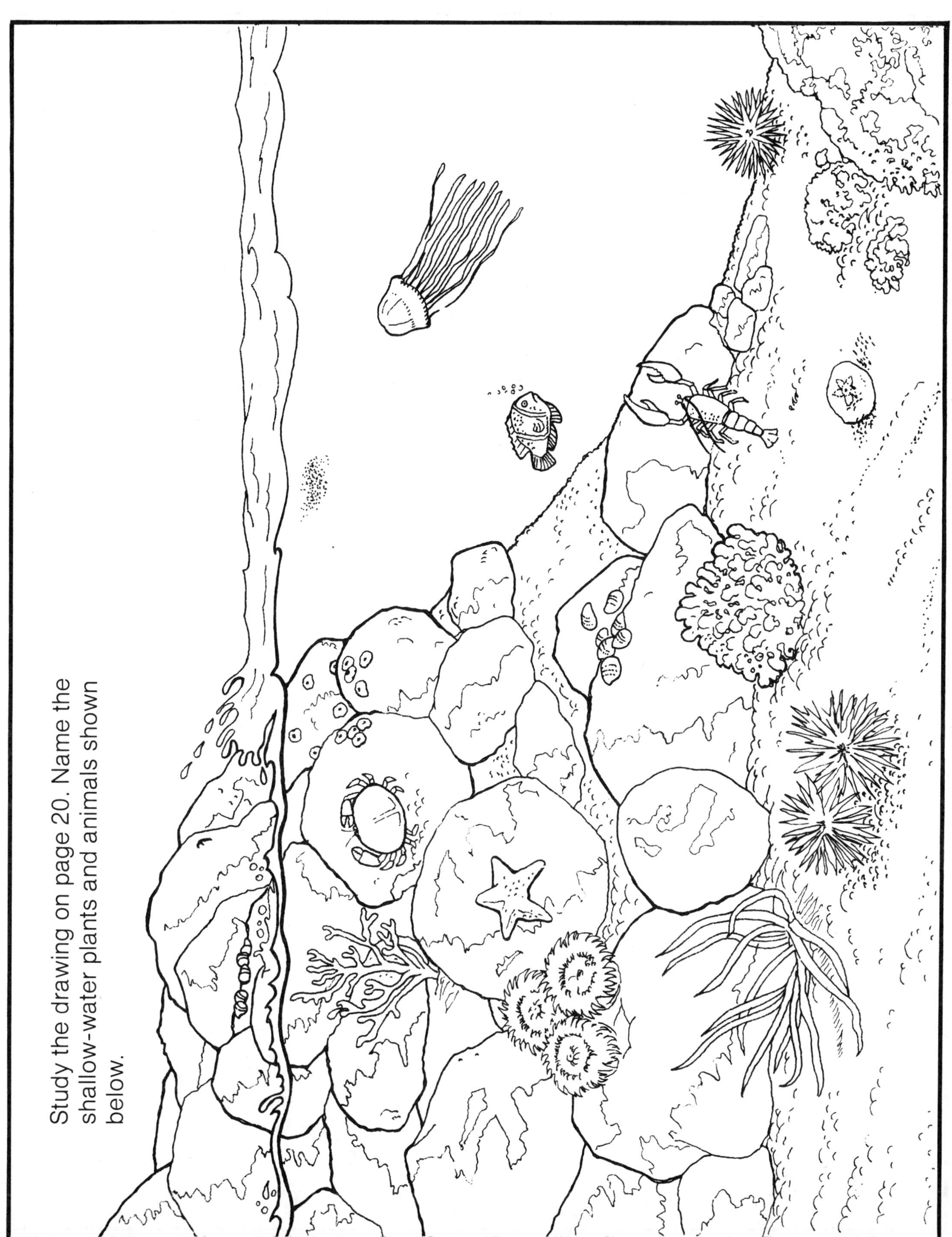

Life in the Ocean—Deep Water

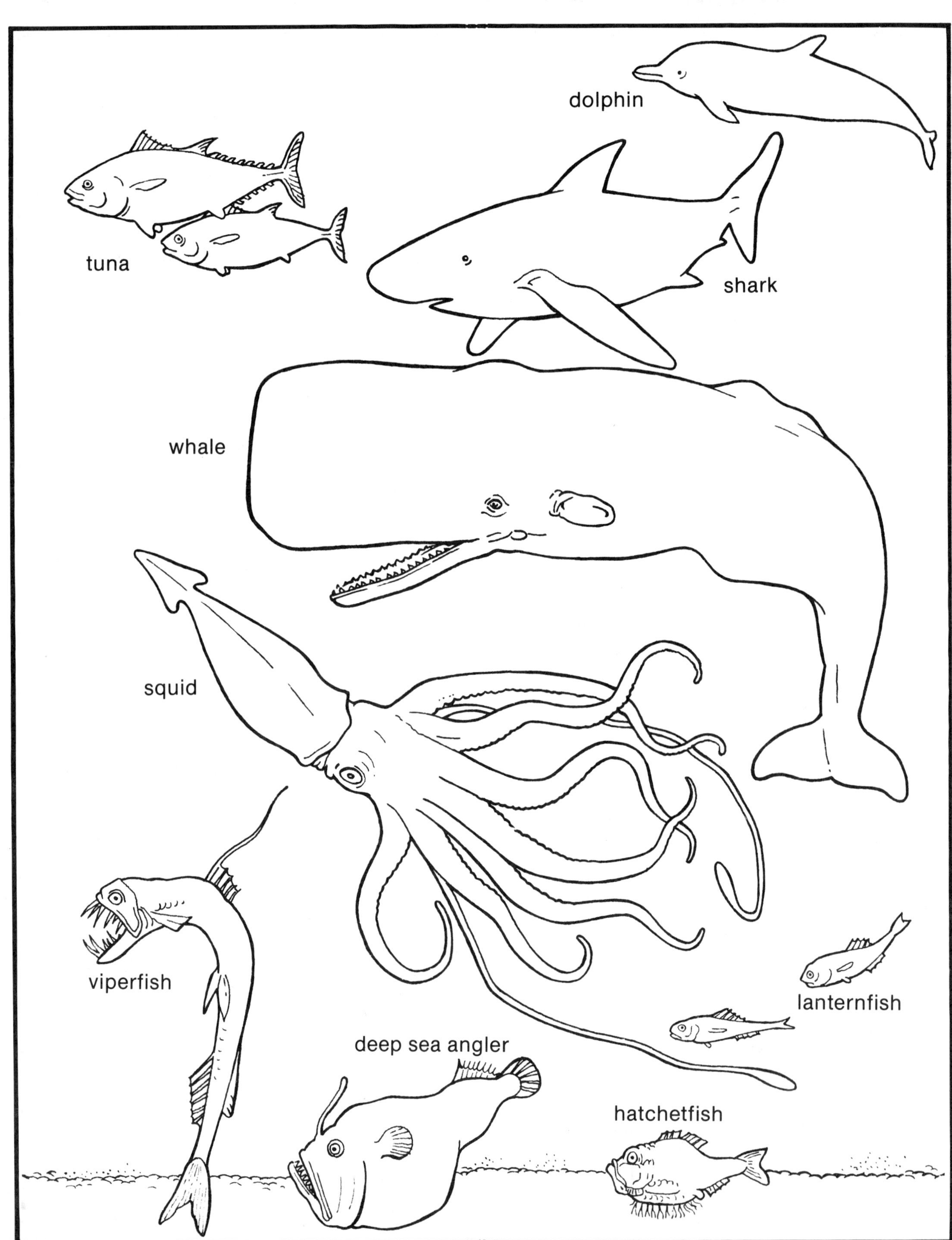

LIFE IN THE OCEAN—DEEP WATER

Study the drawing on page 22. Name the deep-water animals shown below.

REVIEW: OCEAN LIFE

Identify each picture by writing the correct name on the line. Use the letters **S** (shallow) or **D** (deep) to show where in the ocean each would be found. Words to use: plankton, jellyfish, squid, lobster, starfish, seaweed, snails, barnacles, shark, tuna.

1. ____________________ 2. ____________________ 3. ____________________

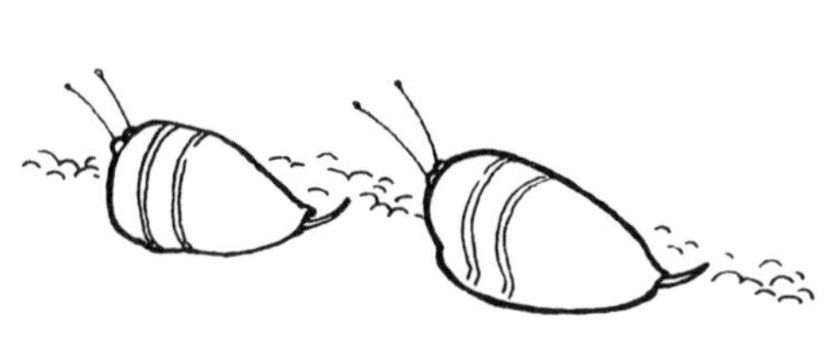

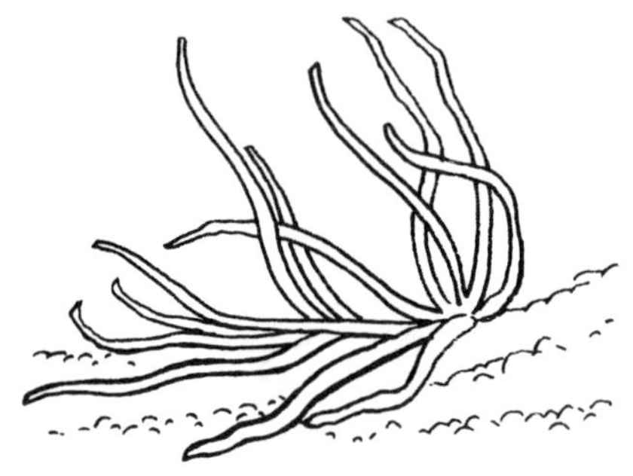

4. ____________________ 5. ____________________ 6. ____________________

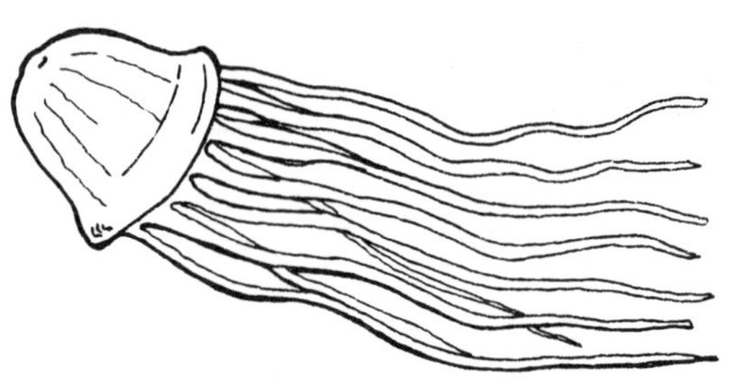

7. ____________________ 8. ____________________

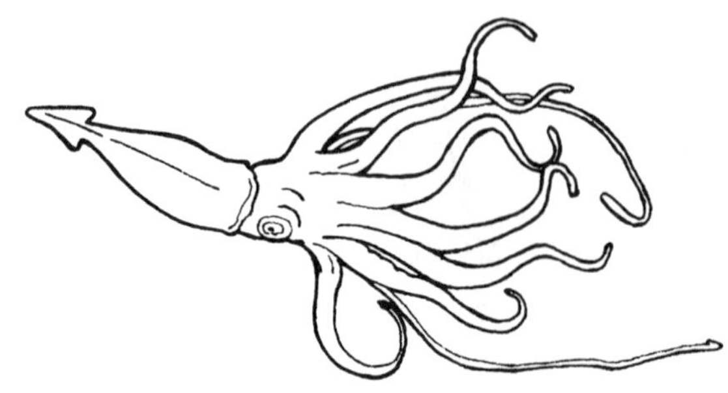

9. ____________________ 10. ____________________

SCUBA

SCUBA is a word formed from the first letters of Self-Contained Underwater Breathing Apparatus. This equipment consists of one or more tanks strapped to a diver's back. These tanks are filled with compressed air and are connected by tubes to a face mask. A valve controls (regulates) the amount of air that enters the mask. For deep dives, the diver also wears a rubber suit and flippers on his feet. An experienced diver can explore near the shore with this equipment down to a depth of about 300 feet. Recent experimental dives have been deeper. Scuba diving has become a hobby for many people. It has not, however, solved the problems of deep-sea diving: air supply and the pressures of deep water.

BATHYSCAPH

Bathyscaphes are deep-diving chambers that make very little horizontal movement. The largest part of the bathyscaph is the float. Certain parts of it are filled with gasoline. Gasoline is lighter than seawater and, therefore, provides buoyancy. The sphere below the float is the scientist's laboratory. There is an entryway leading to it. The sphere is big enough to hold two men, oxygen tanks, and scientific equipment. Portholes permit the scientists to see out. Searchlights illuminate their surroundings. The portholes may be made of plastic about 6 inches thick. The sphere is watertight and has walls of thick steel.

The bathyscaph is made to descend by allowing water to enter some compartments in the float. More water enters as the vessel sinks deeper. Water inside the float also prevents the outside water pressure from crushing the float. Silos on either side of the sphere contain ballast, a heavy material. To make the bathyscaph rise, ballast is released.

UNDERWATER EXPLORATION

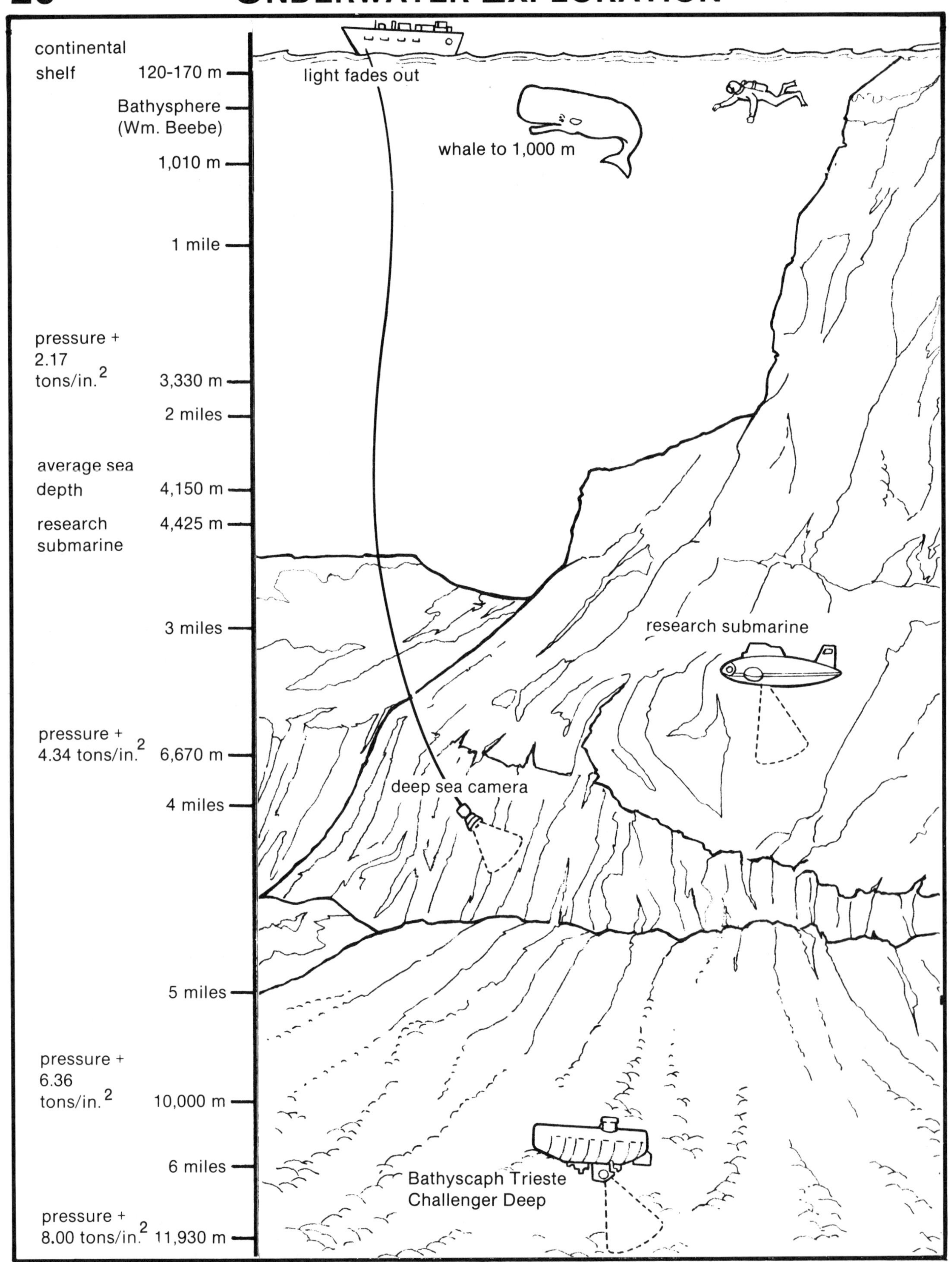

UNDERWATER EXPLORATION

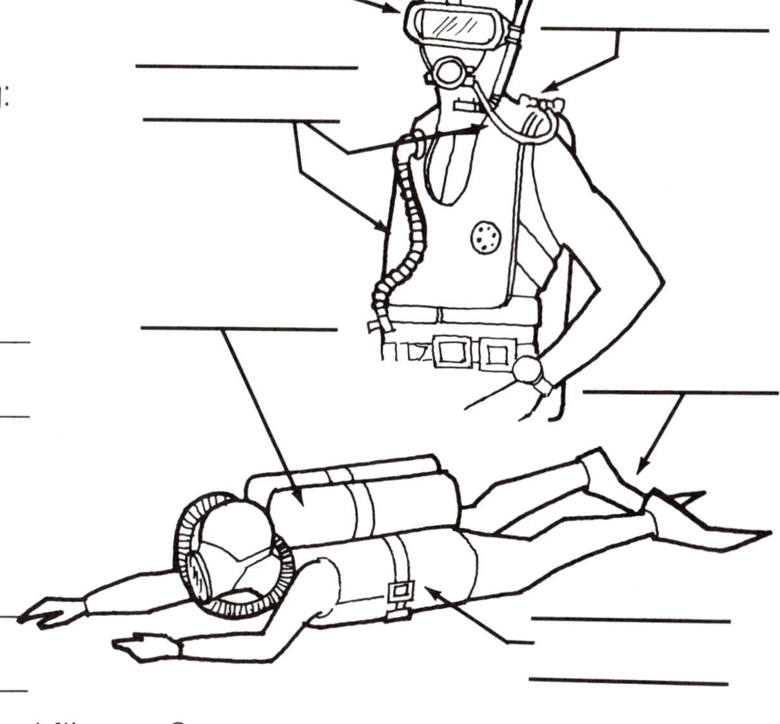

SCUBA

Label the following parts of the drawing: **tank, regulator, connecting tubes, mask, rubber suit, flippers**.

What do the letters SCUBA stand for?

____

____

Why do you think a diver cannot go much below 300 feet with SCUBA equipment?

____

____

What is the purpose of the rubber suit and flippers? ______________________________________

____

BATHYSCAPH

Label the following parts of the drawing: **float, gasoline compartments, sphere, entryway, porthole, silo, searchlight**.

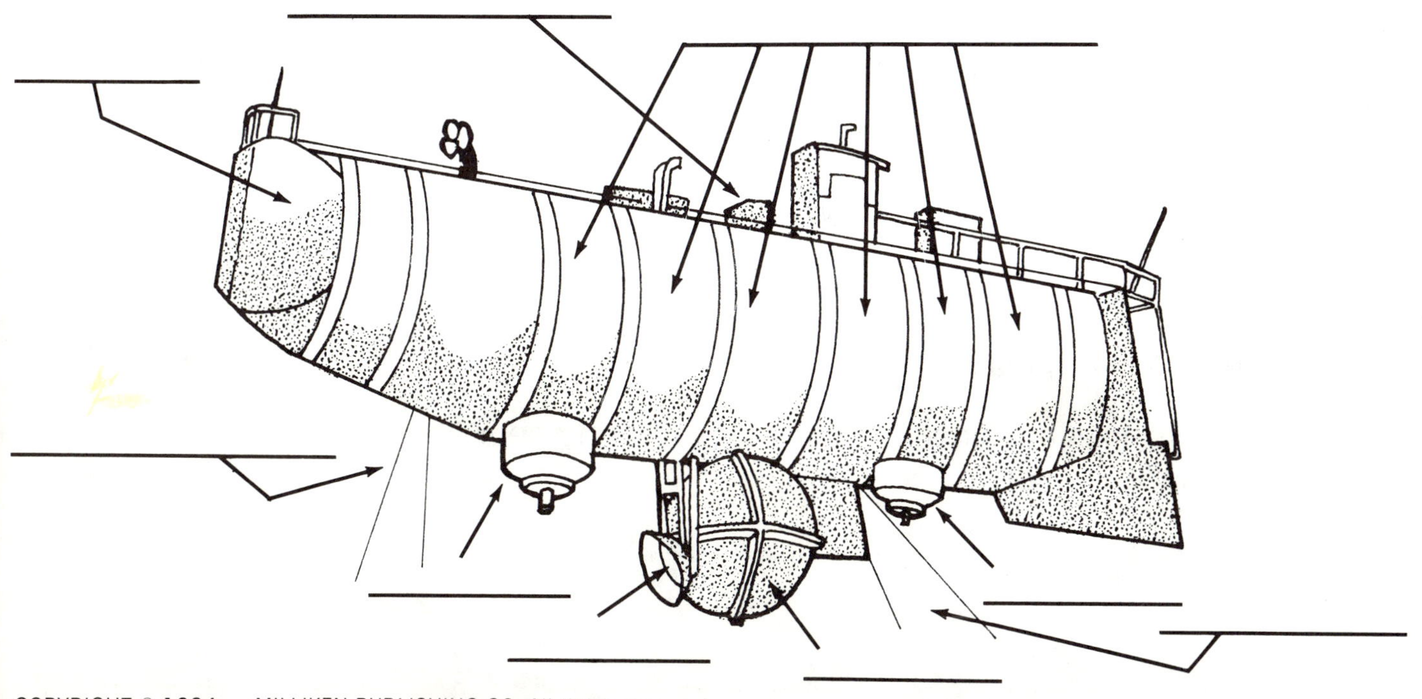

UNDERWATER EXPLORATION

1. Which can go to a greater depth, a SCUBA diver or a bathyscaph?

___

2. What makes a bathyscaph rise in the water? ___

___

3. How does a bathyscaph go lower in the water? ___

___

4. Approximately how deep did the U.S. Navy's bathyscaph, Trieste, dive?

___

5. What is the largest part of a bathyscaph called? ___

TRUE OR FALSE: Circle the correct answer.

1. A bathyscaph has great speed in the water. T F
2. The scientist's laboratory is in the float of a bathyscaph. T F
3. SCUBA divers have been able to explore ocean trenches. T F
4. Bathyscaphes contain portholes. T F
5. Bathyscaphes rise in the water by jet propulsion. T F
6. Ballast is made up of lightweight material. T F
7. SCUBA divers' tanks are filled with compressed air. T F
8. Manned equipment has gone below 10,000 feet. T F
9. A bathyscaph's sphere has walls of thick plastic. T F
10. SCUBA diving is designed primarily for exploring near shore and in shallow water. T F

